Easy Mexican Food Favorites: for kids and Parents

Copyright © 2020. Mary June Smith. All Rights Reserved.

No part of this publication may be reproduced, distributed, or transmitted in any form or by any means, including photocopying, recording, or other electronic or mechanical methods, or by any information storage and retrieval system without the prior written permission of Smith Show Publishing, except in the case of very brief quotations embodied in critical reviews and certain other noncommercial uses permitted by copyright law.

Family meals are fun!

Breastfeeding is the best first family meal.
- Feed your baby only breastmilk the first 6 months.
- Breastfeed as long as you and baby want.

Start little ones at the table early.
- Children as young as 6 months can sit in a highchair during meal time.
- Young children and infants over 6 months can eat small bites of soft foods from the family table.

Cook meals quickly and eat slowly.
- Parents decide what foods to serve and children decide how much to eat.
- Older children can help prepare meals.
- Children are more likely to eat if they help cook.

Have family meals with your children.
- Children of all ages eat better when adults eat with them.
- Mom and Dad and other adults are role models for healthy eating.

Talk to each other at the table.
- Share the best part of the day, what is going on or family stories.
- Save serious talk for another time.
- Turn off the TV during meals.

How to get your child to try healthy foods

Some children may be picky eaters, a parent's responsibility is to provide a positive eating atmosphere and healthy food choices.

Tips to get them to eat healthy foods

- **Give foods silly names.**
- **Let children help** with shopping and cooking.
- **Go easy on sugar and salt**—gradually reduce the amount you use. If your child is raised without as much sugar and salt they won't miss it. Try to use honey instead of sugar because it is sweeter so you need less. Avoid honey for first year.
- **Teach your child about basic nutrition**—talk with your child about eating healthy foods and why. Try playing games.
- **Serve in small helpings and bite size**—smaller amounts are best. If your child wants more he or she will ask for more.
- **Ask your child to try everything, but don't force them to finish.**
- **Do not give your child snacks in the hour before mealtime**—eating too soon before meals will fill your child up and he or she won't get nutrients needed from meal time foods.
- **Be creative**—children love bright colors, animals and funny shapes. Serve food on different plates or cut food into shapes.
- **Make mealtime fun and social**—keep eating a positive experience for your child and it can be a fun time for the whole family. Do not watch TV while eating. Avoid nagging, threatening or begging your child to eat something. It is your responsibility to offer healthy food, but your child needs to choose what and how much they want to eat.
- **Eat the same foods as your child**—children learn by example. If they see you eating it then they know it must be good. Don't share your food dislikes with your child.

Cooking with Children

There are many reasons to cook with your children:

- You, your children and other family members (including Dad) spend time together
- Your children will not be in front of the TV
- Your children learn about the importance of eating healthy
- Your children are more likely to eat food they helped prepare
- Your children develop their brain and thinking skills
- Children learn to follow directions
- It is an opportunity to praise your children
- It gives children a feeling of accomplishment
- Your children learn important life skills
- You and your children are having fun!!!

How to Cook with Children

1. **Wash hands.**
2. Decide on the **area of the kitchen** where you will work.
3. **Gather stools or chairs** that will allow your child to stand or sit comfortably while working.
4. Get out the **recipe** you will be using.
5. **Read** the recipe with your child. Explain that you will be following the steps in the recipe to prepare the food.
6. Set out:
   - **equipment and supplies** that you will need
   - **ingredients** that you will be using.
7. **Have your child help with cooking activities.**
8. **Clean up** with your child.
9. **Eat** what you have prepared.

What Can Young Children Do?

Your child can help. How wil depend on her or his age. Keep the following in mind with young children and cooking:

2-year-olds are learning to use the large muscles in their arms:

- scrub vegetables and fruits
- carry unbreakable items to the table
- dip foods
- wash and tear lettuce and salad greens
- break bread into pieces

3 year-olds are learning to use their hands:

- pour liquids into batter (you measure first)
- mix batter or other dry and wet ingredients together
- shake a drink in a closed container
- spread butters or spreads
- knead dough
- wash vegetables and fruit
- serve foods
- put things in the trash after cooking or after a meal

4 & 5-year-olds are learning to control small muscles in their fingers:

- squeeze or juice oranges, lemons, and limes
- peel some fruits and vegetables (bananas, onions, etc.)
- mash soft fruits and vegetables
- cut soft foods with a plastic knife (mushrooms, hard-boiled eggs)
- press cookie cutters
- measure dry ingredients
- crack open/ break eggs
- beat eggs with an egg beater
- set the table
- wipe up after cooking
- clear the table after a meal

Safety Tips for Cooking with Children

1. Prevent food poisoning by:
    - Always washing hands before cooking.
    - Not eating raw eggs or raw meats.
    - Waiting until the food is cooked before sampling it.
    - No sampling uncooked foods.
    - Keeping refrigerated foods cool until use.
    - Using fresh ingredients, watch expiration dates.

2. Have children stand at the level of the activity. Use a stool if necessary.

3. Keep children away from the stove or oven when turned on and let food cool a little before serving to children.

4. Use cooking supplies that will not break (such as plastic measuring cups and stainless-steel bowls).

5. Use plastic knives or butter knives for cutting.

6. Always watch everything your children do.
    - Always watch children when they use knives, mixers, or the stove.
    - Supervise the use of ovens, stoves, and other kitchen appliances.
    - Remind children that stoves, ovens, pans, and dishes can be very hot.

What to expect from children and their cooking

- It will be messy.
- It will take longer than when done by a parent alone.
- The finished product might not look pretty.
- They will be very proud of themselves! So praise them.
- You will have an opportunity to praise them.

Cooking with Beans

Four Easy Steps for Cooking Beans

1. **BUY GOOD BEANS**
   Look for clean, firm, whole beans of the same color and size.

2. **WASH and SORT**
   Get rid of foreign objects and damaged beans. Rinse in cold water.

3. **SOAK**
   For every pound (2 cups) beans, add 10 cups hot water in a large pot. Boil 2-3 minutes, then cover and soak 4 –12 hours. Drain off soaking water and rinse.

4. **COOK**
   Put beans, soaked, drained and rinsed, (1 lb. dry make 4-6 cups cooked) into a large pot with 6 cups of water. Boil gently until desired tenderness (depends on type of bean, usually 1-2 hours). You want firmer beans for salads and softer beans for mashing.

Storage Tips

Store dry beans in a cool, dry place in a tightly closed container.

Cooking Tips

Beans are a complimentary food and go well with many different flavors (add your favorite spices or sauces). Try adding beans to your favorite casseroles or dishes. Beans are an exciting addition to boring salads. Mashed beans are good added to ground meat for burgers or instead of tuna for a sandwich spread. Pureed beans added to soups make them heartier.

Pre-cooking Beans

Cooking a bunch of beans ahead of time is a good idea. Cooked beans will keep for 4-5 days in the refrigerator and 4-5 months in the freezer. Try putting them in small yogurt containers. Pull them out and pop them in any meal or dish.

Microwaves are an excellent way to reheat beans.

- 1 cup of uncooked dry beans when cooked is equivalent to 1 can of beans.

- Beans are a great soft table food for infants when mashed and whole for older children.

Salad   beans, cheese

Pasta Salad with Veggies

4 servings, about 1 1/2 cups each

Ingredients

- 2 cups cooked pasta
- 2 cups chopped, cooked vegetables (broccoli, carrots, etc.)
- **1 cup garbanzo beans*,** cooked and drained
- **1/2 cup cubed or shredded cheddar cheese***
- 1 clove garlic, minced or 1/8 teaspoon garlic powder
- 1 tomato, diced
- 1/2-1 cup low-fat Italian vinaigrette salad dressing, as desired

*WIC food

Steps

1. y In a bowl, mix all ingredients together.
2. y Cool in refrigerator until ready to serve.
3. y To serve, top salad with cheddar cheese.

y   Steps for Children

Soup   lentils, milk

Leo the Leopard's Lentil Soup

6 servings, about 2 cups each

Ingredients

1 tbsp vegetable oil 1
cup chopped onion

2 cups dried lentils*, rinsed

3 cup chopped carrots
4 cups diced tomatoes, fresh or canned (14 oz)
8 cups water or broth/stock

1 cup shredded Mozzarella cheese*

*WIC food

Steps

1. In large pot, heat oil over medium heat. Cook onion in oil until soft and lightly browned (about 5 minutes).
2. Add lentils, carrots, and tomatoes.
3. Add water. Stir.
4. Bring ingredients to a boil.
5. Reduce heat to low and simmer for about 45 minutes or until lentils are tender.
6. Spoon soup into bowls. Top with cheese.

Small meals   beans, cheese

Quesadillas

Makes 6 pieces

Ingredients

- 2 small tortillas
- **1/4 cup mashed beans***
- **1/2 cup shredded cheddar cheese***
- salsa, if desired

WIC food

Steps

1. Spread 2 tbsp beans onto each tortilla.
2. Sprinkle cheese over beans.
3. Put another tortilla on top of bean-cheese mixture.
4. Heat frying pan over medium heat.
5. Place tortilla "sandwich" in pan. Cook for about 1 minute on first side until golden brown, then flip over. Cook for about 1 minute on second side until golden brown and cheese has melted.
6. Remove from pan and cut into 6 triangular pieces, like you would a pizza. Serve with salsa, if desired.

Small Meals   beans, cheese

Nachos

4 servings, about 2 cups each

Ingredients

- 1 (7 oz) bag tortilla chips
- **2 cups cooked mashed pinto beans* or refried beans**
- **1 1/2 cups shredded cheddar cheese***
- 3 tomato, chopped
- 4 green onions, chopped
- 1 cup salsa
- 1/2 cup sour cream or plain yogurt

*WIC food

Steps

1. Put chips in large greased baking dish and cover with beans and cheese.
2. Put baking dish in oven under broiler for 5 minutes or until cheese has melted.
3. Top with onions, tomatoes, salsa, and sour cream or plain yogurt.

Side Dishes   beans, milk

Refried Beans

Makes about 5 cups

Ingredients

   1 pound dried pinto beans*
   water, as needed
   2 cloves garlic, minced or 1/4 teaspoon garlic powder
   3 tbsp finely chopped onion
   2 tbsp vegetable oil
   1/2 cup milk*
   1/4 cup chopped cilantro (optional)

WIC food

Steps

1. y Put beans in pot.
2. y Rinse with water. Drain.
3. y Cover beans with fresh water (about 1 inch above beans).
4. Cover pot. Bring to a gentle boil. Cook until beans are soft (about 1 to 2 hours or longer if using crock pot). Add water as needed to keep beans covered with liquid.
5. Once beans are soft, pour off water and set aside.
6. In frying pan, cook garlic and onion in oil until soft and lightly browned (about 5 minutes). Add to beans.
7. y Mash beans with fork.
8. y Stir in milk until desired thickness.

Small Meal   beans, eggs, cheese

Burritos

Makes 4 burritos

Ingredients

    2 cups filling (cooked ground meat, **scrambled eggs* and beans***)
    4 small flour or corn tortillas
    1/2 cup chopped lettuce
    1/2 cup chopped tomatoes

    1/2 cup shredded cheddar cheese*

    1/2 cup salsa

*WIC food

Steps

1. Cook filling.
2. Heat tortillas
3. Spoon 1/2 cup of filling, 1 tbsp each of tomato, lettuce, cheese, and salsa onto each tortilla.
4. Roll up tortilla.

Main Dish   beans, cheese

Little Red Riding Hood's Chili

6 servings, about 2 cups each

Ingredients

- 1/2 -1 pound ground meat (beef, turkey, wild game, etc.)
- **2 cups cooked pinto or kidney beans***
- 1 (14 oz) can tomatoes (whole, diced, or crushed)
- 1/2 cup chopped onion
- 1 cup chopped green pepper
- 3 cups water or broth/stock
- 1 tsp chili powder
- **1/2 cup cheese, grated***

*WIC food

Steps

1. In large pot, brown ground meat and drain off fat.
2. Add beans, tomatoes, onion, green pepper, stock (or water) and spices to meat. Stir.
3. Bring mixture to a boil. Reduce heat. Cover and cook over low heat for about 10-15 minutes.
4. . y   Sprinkle cheese over the top

Cereal

What to do with cereal

Cereal in the traditional way is always good: cereal with milk.

- Try adding fruit (fresh, frozen or canned.)

But, if you don't like cereal with milk try:

- Sprinkle WIC cereal over desserts or breakfast meals like oatmeal.
- Sprinkle WIC cereal over casseroles for a crunchy top.
- Crushed cereal is good in breads or baked goods. It also makes a good crust or bottom for dessert bars.
- Add to snack mixes for extra crunch.
- Crushed cereal with spices is good as a breading for fish or chicken— just use milk or eggs for make it stick.

Storage Tips:

- Store cereal in a cool, dry place in a sealed container.

Breakfast/Snack   cereal

Breakfast Banana Split

2 servings, about 1 cup each

Ingredients

   1 banana, peeled
   1 cup vanilla yogurt
   1/2 cup cereal*

WIC food

Steps

1. Cut banana into quarters lengthwise (from top to bottom).
2. Put 2 banana pieces in each bowl.
3. Spoon yogurt into bowl between banana halves.
4. Top yogurt with cereal.

Breakfast   cereal, milk, eggs

Cereal Fruit Pancakes

Makes 8 servings

Ingredients

- 1 1/2 cups all-purpose flour
- 2 tbsp sugar
- 1 tbsp baking powder
- **1 egg***
- **2 cups milk ***
- 2 tbsp vegetable oil
- **1 cup corn flakes cereal***
- 1 cup cubed fruit (strawberries, apples, or blueberries, etc.)

*WIC food

Steps

1. Stir together flour, sugar and baking powder. Set aside.
2. In large mixing bowl, beat egg until foamy. Stir in milk, vegetable oil and cereal. Let stand 2 minutes or until cereal softens.
3. Add flour mixture, stirring to combine. Batter will be lumpy.
4. Add fruit and mix.
5. Portion batter, using 1/4 cup for each pancake, onto preheated greased griddle. Turn once, cooking until golden brown on both sides. Serve hot.

Bread   cereal, milk, eggs

Honey of a Muffin

Makes 12 muffins

Ingredients

　　1 1/3 cups flour

　　1/2 cup sugar

　　1 tbsp. baking powder

　　1 egg*

　　1 cup milk *

　　1/3 cup butter or margarine, melted

　　1 /2 cups Post Honey Bunches of Oats Cereal*

*WIC food

Steps

1. Preheat oven to 400°F.
2. y   Mix flour, sugar and baking powder in large bowl.
3. y   Beat egg in small bowl. Stir in milk and butter.
4. y   Add to flour mixture; stir just until moistened. (Batter will be lumpy.)
5. y   Stir in cereal.
6. y   Spoon batter into greased or paper-lined muffin pan, filling each cup 2/3 full.
7. Bake 20 minutes or until golden brown. Serve warm.

Main Dish   cereal, cheese, milk, eggs

Baked Chicken

Makes 6 servings

Ingredients

    3 cups crispy rice cereal (crushed 3/4 cup)*

    1/3 cup cheese*

    2 eggs*

    1/3 cup milk*

    1/3 cup all-purpose flour

    1/2 tsp thyme (optional)

    1 tsp basil (optional)

    Or other seasonings

    6 boneless, skinless, chicken pieces

*WIC food

Steps

1. Combine the crispy rice cereal and cheese in shallow pan or plate. Set aside.
2. In small mixing bowl, beat egg and milk slightly.
3. Add flour and spices. Mix until smooth.
4. Dip chicken in batter.
5. Coat with cereal mixture.
6. Place in single layer in shallow baking pan coated with cooking spray.
7. Bake at 350° F about 55 minutes or until chicken is tender, no longer pink and juices run clear. Do not cover pan or turn chicken while baking. Serve hot.

Main Dish   cereal, cheese

Spaghetti with Meatballs

6 servings, about 1 1/2 cups each

Ingredients

    1 lb lean ground meat (beef, turkey or wild game)
    1/2 cup crushed cornflake cereal*
    1 egg*, beaten
    1/2 cup shredded cheddar cheese*
    2 cups cooked spaghetti noodles
    1 clove garlic, minced or 1/8 teaspoon garlic powder
    1 tsp oregano (optional)
    1/2 tsp basil (optional)
    1 tsp thyme (optional) 1
    tbsp vegetable oil
    1 (28 oz) can or 2 (14 oz) cans of crushed tomatoes
    1 (12 oz) can or 2 (6 oz) cans of tomato paste
    1 cup water OR 1 jar spaghetti sauce

WIC food

Steps

1. Preheat oven to 350°F.
2. . y In large bowl, combine meat, cereal, egg, and cheese.
3. . y With hands, form into small balls.
4. Put meatballs onto baking sheet. Bake for about 10 minutes and then turn meatballs over.
5. Bake for another 10 minutes.
6. In large saucepan, brown garlic in oil. Add tomatoes, tomato paste, and water. Stir. Bring to a boil. Reduce heat and simmer for 15 minutes or longer if desired. OR heat sauce. Serve meatballs and sauce over cooked spaghetti.

Main Dish   cereal, eggs, milk

Meat Loaf

Makes 12 servings

Ingredients 1

cup milk*

2 eggs*

3 cups Shredded Wheat Cereal, crushed*

1 can (8 oz.) stewed tomatoes

1 medium onion, chopped

1/4 cup chopped green pepper

2 tsp Worcestershire sauce

1/4 tsp ground black pepper

2 lb. ground meat (beef, turkey, wild game, etc.)

*WIC food

Steps

1 . y   Mix milk and eggs in large bowl.

2 . y   Mix cereal, tomatoes, onion, green pepper, Worcestershire sauce, black pepper and ground meat.

3 . y   Shape meat mixture into oval loaf in shallow baking pan.

4. Bake at 375°F for 1 hour or until cooked through (160°F).

y   Steps for Children

Dessert   cereal, eggs, milk

Carrot Cake

CAKE
- 1 cup regular all-purpose flour
- 1 1/2 tsp baking powder
- 1 tsp ground cinnamon
- 1/8 tsp ground ginger
- **2 eggs***
- 1 cup firmly packed brown sugar
- 1/4 cup vegetable oil
- **1/4 cup creamy peanut butter***
- 1 1/2 cups grated raw carrots
- **2 cups Raisin Bran cereal***
- 1/2 cup chopped walnuts

FROSTING:
- 2 cups powdered sugar
- 4 oz cream cheese
- 1 tsp vanilla extract
- **2 tsp milk***

*WIC food

CAKE
1. Stir together flour, baking powder, cinnamon and ginger. Set aside.
2. In large mixing bowl, beat eggs slightly.
3. Stir in sugar, peanut butter and oil.
4. Add carrots and cereal. Mix well. Let stand 10 minutes.
5. Add flour mixture and walnuts. Mix until well combined.
6. Pour into greased 8 x 8 x 2-inch baking pan.
7. Bake in oven at 350° F about 45 minutes or until wooden pick inserted near center comes out clean. Cool completely.

FROSTING
1. In electric mixer bowl, beat frosting ingredients until smooth and creamy.
2. Spread on cooled cake.

The secrets of cheese

- Cheese tastes good with breads, crackers, meats, beans, pastas, rice, eggs & vegetables.

- Sliced cheese is an excellent snack on bread, cold or melted, crackers or sandwiches.

- Shredded or grated cheese is great sprinkled on top of casseroles, soups, salads, cooked vegetables & rice, potato, pasta or bean dishes.

- A little shredded cheese is good for children after 9 months.

Storage Tips

- Always refrigerate, wrap well to prevent mold & drying out.

- If it molds, cut away the moldy spots & use the rest as soon as possible.

- If it is dry, crumble or grate & sprinkle on casseroles, etc. as soon as possible.

Freezing Cheese

- Wrap cheese in plastic wrap then put into a freezer bag. It will last up to 4 months in the freezer and a couple weeks after thawed. Thaw in the refrigerator. It will crumble easily. Use like shredded cheese.

Salad cheese

Apple Cheddar Salad

Serves 4

Ingredients

DRESSING

- 1/4 cup lemon juice
- 2 tbsp honey
- 1 tsp vegetable oil

SALAD

- 4 cups chopped apples
- **1/2 cup cubed cheddar cheese***
- 3 cups mixed salad greens

*WIC food

Steps

1. y   To prepare dressing, combine first three ingredients in a small bowl, stirring well with a whisk.
2. y   To prepare salad, combine apples and cheese.
3. y   Drizzle dressing over apple mixture; toss gently to coat. Serve over greens.

y   Steps for Children

Small Meals   cheese

Mini Pizzas

Makes 4 pizzas

Ingredients

- 1/2 cup tomato sauce
- 2 English muffins or bagels, sliced in halves
- **1/2 cup shredded Mozzarella cheese***
- 1 cup diced vegetables (such as zucchini, broccoli, green pepper, mushrooms, tomatoes, or onion)

WIC food

Steps

1. Preheat oven to 350°F.
2. y   Spread tomato sauce on each muffin/bagel half and sprinkle with cheese.
3. y   Top with vegetables.
4. y   Place on cookie/baking sheet.
5. Bake for about 10 minutes or until cheese has melted.

y   Steps for Children

Side Dish   cheese, milk, eggs

Mr. Potato Head's Scalloped Potatoes

4 servings, about 1 cup each

Ingredients

- 1 tsp vegetable oil
- 3 cups washed and sliced potatoes
- 1 cup sliced onions
- **1/2 cup milk***
- 2 tsp flour
- **1/4 cup shredded cheddar cheese***
- 1 tsp pepper

*WIC food

Steps

1. Preheat oven to 375°F.
2. y Grease an 8-by-8-inch baking dish with oil.
3. y Layer half of potatoes into baking dish. Cover with onions. Add remaining potatoes.
4. y Mix flour with milk until smooth
5. y Pour milk over potato-onion mixture. Top with cheese. Season with pepper.
6. Cover and bake for about 50 minutes. Uncover and bake for another 10 minutes.

y   Steps for Children

Side Dish   cheese

Cheesy Potato Patties

Makes 12-15 patties

Ingredients

  6 large potatoes, washed and quartered

  1 cup cheddar cheese, grated*

  2 cups cooked vegetables (carrots, broccoli, zucchini, etc)

  flour (to cover)

  1 tbsp butter

*WIC food

Steps

1. Place potatoes in saucepan of boiling water and cook until soft, about 25 minutes.

2. y   Drain and mash potatoes and leave to cool.

3. Cut vegetables into tiny pieces.

4. y   When potatoes are cool, add cheese and vegetables then mix

5. y   Roll mixture into patties and flour lightly.

6. Heat butter in a pan. Fry patties until brown and crispy about 3 to 5 minutes on each side.

y   Steps for Children

Main Dish　　　　　　　　　　　　　　　　　　　　　　cheese

Noodly Tuna Bake

Makes about 9 (2 1/2-by-2 1/2-inch) pieces

Ingredients

- 1 tsp vegetable oil
- 2 (6 oz) cans of tuna, packed in water, drained (or canned salmon)
- 3 cups egg noodles, cooked
- 3 (14 oz) can of whole kernel corn
- 4 cups thinly sliced zucchini squash
- **1/2 cup shredded cheddar cheese***
- **1/2 cup crushed cereal***

*WIC food

Steps

Preheat oven to 350°F.

y Grease 8-by-8-inch baking dish with oil.

y In bowl, mix tuna, noodles, corn, and zucchini.

y Spoon mixture into baking dish.

y Top with cheese and cereal.

Bake for about 50 minutes or until hot and bubbly.

y Steps for Children

Main Dish   cheese

Veggie Lasagna

Makes about 12 pieces

Ingredients

- 1 tsp vegetable oil
- 3 cups low-fat cottage cheese
- 1 (10 oz) package frozen vegetables thawed and drained
- 1 (8 oz) package of lasagna noodles, uncooked
- **1 cup shredded Mozzarella cheese***

- 1 (6 oz) can tomato paste
- 1 (28 oz) or 2 (15 oz) cans of diced tomatoes
- 1 tsp oregano
- 1 clove garlic, minced or 1/8 teaspoon garlic powder
- OR
- 1 jar spaghetti sauce

*WIC food

Steps

1. Preheat oven to 375°F.
2. Grease 9-by-13-inch baking dish with oil.
3. In bowl, mix cottage cheese and spinach (or broccoli) together.
4. In another bowl, mix together tomato paste, tomatoes, oregano, and garlic to make sauce.
5. Layer ingredients into baking dish: Start with half of sauce, then half of noodles, all of cottage cheese-vegetable mixture, other half of noodles, and other half of sauce. Top with Mozzarella cheese.
6. Cover dish with aluminum foil. Bake for 1 hour. Uncover and bake for another 15 minutes until lightly browned on top and bubbling.

Main Dish   cheese, milk

Quick Macaroni & Cheese with Veggies

Serves 6

Ingredients

4 cups water

1 1/2 cups uncooked macaroni

1 egg, beaten* 1

1/2 cups milk*

1/2 lb cheese, shredded*

1 tsp chopped onion

1 cup cooked, chopped vegetables

*WIC food

Steps

1. Bring water to boil and add macaroni.
2. Cook 10 minutes, stir occasionally.
3. Drain macaroni and set aside.
4. y Combine egg, milk, cheese, and onion in a bowl.
5. y Combine with macaroni.
6. Cook over low heat until cheese melts, keep stirring to avoid sticking.
7. y Add vegetables. Serve right away.

y   Steps for Children

Eggs

Using Eggs

- Eggs make great breakfasts, lunches or dinners as fried, poached, scrambled, deviled or in an omelet with vegetables, meat & cheese.

- Eggs are great in casseroles, ground meat (burgers), baked goods, salads & sandwiches

- Infants can have mashed yolks at 8 months & whites after 1 year.

Storage Tips

- Always keep eggs refrigerated in their carton. For every hour eggs are at room temperature they age a day. The older the eggs, the higher the risk for food poisoning. Do not eat raw eggs.

Freezing Eggs

Eggs that are frozen in the correct way are perfectly fine to eat and bake with. They last up to 6 months in the freezer.

Whole Eggs - beat the yolk & white together, then put into a freezing container & label with the number of eggs & the date.

Yolks - yolks are special: in the freezer yolks become too similar to gelatin so add 1/8 tsp salt or 1 1/2 tsp sugar for every 1/4 cup (4 yolks). Put into a freezer container and label with number of eggs, date and whether it has salt (for main dishes) or sugar (for desserts or baked goods).

Thaw eggs in the refrigerator and use as soon as thawed

For use after thawing

- Use 3 tbsp of whole egg for every fresh egg
- Use 1 tbsp yolk for every fresh yolk
- Use 2 tbsp whites for every fresh white

Breakfast   eggs, milk, cheese

Humpty Dumpty's Omelet

Makes about 8 servings

Ingredients

- 2 tsp vegetable oil
- 1 small onion, minced
- 2 cups chopped spinach or other greens
- 2 cups other chopped vegetables (such as peppers, broccoli, carrots, etc)
- 1/4 cup water
- **6 eggs***
- **1/2 cup milk***
- **1 cup shredded cheese***

WIC food

Steps

1. Preheat oven to 375°F.
2. Grease 8-by-8-inch baking dish with 1 tsp oil.
3. In large frying pan, cook onion in 1 tsp oil until soft and brown.
4. Cook vegetables until soft.
5. Remove vegetables and set aside.
6. Stir in spinach and water. Cover and cook for about 5 minutes.
7. In large bowl mix together eggs, milk, and cheeses. Add in onion, vegetables and spinach. Stir. Pour mixture into baking dish.
8. Bake for about 35 minutes until slightly browned on top and firm to the touch.

Breakfast   eggs, milk

Fruity French Toast

Makes 8 slices

Ingredients

4 eggs*

1/2 cup milk*

8 slices of bread

4 tsp butter or margarine

2 cups sliced fruit (such as bananas, apples, peaches etc.)

*WIC food

Steps

1. y In bowl, beat eggs and milk together.
2. y Dip bread into egg mixture so bread is thoroughly soaked.
3. Coat frying pan with 1 teaspoon butter or margarine and place over medium heat.
4. Put 2 bread slices in pan and heat until lightly browned. Turn slices over and heat until browned. Repeat until all bread slices have been browned. (Use 1 tsp of butter or margarine for every 2 slices of bread.)
5. y Top each bread slice with sliced fruit.

y   Steps for Children

Side Dish   eggs

Quick and Easy Fried Rice

Serves 6

Ingredients

- 3 cups cooked brown or white rice
- 2 cups of frozen vegetables or fresh cooked, cubed vegetables
- 1 small onion chopped
- 1 cup cooked poultry, fish or meat (optional)
- **2 eggs, lightly beaten***
- 3 tsp vegetable oil
- 4 tsp soy sauce

*WIC food

Steps

1. In a large pan, heat oil on high heat. Add onion and rice. Stir and cook until onion is soft, about 5 minutes.

2. Reduce heat to medium and add vegetables and meat to rice mixture then cook 2 minutes.

3. Remove rice and vegetable mixture and set aside.

4. Scramble the eggs in the same pan until cooked form. Mix the eggs with the rice and vegetables then sprinkle with soy sauce.

Bread eggs

Southern Cornbread

Makes 12 muffins, corn sticks, or pieces

Ingredients

    2 cups cornmeal
    1 1/2 tsp baking powder
    1/2 tsp baking soda
    2 tbsp sugar, optional
    1 1/2 cups buttermilk (or **1 1/2 cups milk*** and 1 tbsp vinegar)
    1 egg*, lightly beaten or powdered
    2 tbsp vegetable oil

*WIC food

Steps

1. Preheat oven to 450° F.
2. y   In bowl, mix dry ingredients together.
3. y   Stir in buttermilk and egg, stirring until just moistened.
4. Heat oil in 9-inch cast iron skillet or pan, muffin tin, or corn stick mold until hot. Pour in mixture and bake until golden brown (about 30 minutes for skillet, 15 minutes for muffins or corn sticks).

y   Steps for Children

Main Dish   egg, milk

Vegetable Egg Pie

Serves 6

Ingredients

- 1 9 inch pie shell (or no shell at all just grease the pan)
- 1 cup vegetables, cooked, drained
- **1/2 cup shredded cheese***
- **1 1/2 cups dry egg mix* and 1 1/2 cups water (or 12 fresh eggs stirred with a fork)***
- **1 cup milk***
- 1 1/2 cup water
- 2 tbsp onion
- 1/2 tsp oregano (optional)

*WIC food

Steps

1. Prick bottom and side of pie shell with a fork.
2. Bake at 450 degrees until light brown (5 minutes).
3. Sprinkle vegetables and cheese into pie shell.
4. Beat egg mix with remaining ingredients until well mixed.
5. Pour over cheese.
6. Bake at 375 degrees for 30 – 35 minute. Let stand 5 minutes before serving.

Main Dish   egg, milk, cheese

Strata

Serves 8

Use your favorite sausages, bread, cheese and vegetables in this versatile breakfast casserole recipe.

Ingredients

- 10 bread slices, cubed
- 1 lb. sausage, cooked and drained
- 2 cups frozen, canned or fresh cooked vegetable (such as carrots, peas, mushrooms, asparagus, etc)
- **2 cups grated cheddar cheese***
- 2 tbsp. flour
- 1 tbsp. dry mustard
- 2 tsp dried basil leaves (optional)
- 1/2 tsp salt
- 2 tbsp. melted butter
- **8 eggs***
- **3 cups milk***

*WIC food

Steps

1. Preheat oven 350 degrees.
2. Grease 13x9" glass baking dish.
3. Layer 1/2 of bread, cooked sausage, vegetables and cheese in dish.
4. Repeat layers, ending with cheese.
5. In large bowl, combine remaining ingredients and beat well to mix.
6. Pour over layers in baking dish. Cover tightly and refrigerate overnight.
7. In the morning, preheat oven to 350 degrees.
8. Bake casserole for 60 to 70 minutes until puffed and light golden

To juice or not to juice?

Juice is a good snack, but too much can cause...

- Tooth decay
- Stomach problems
- Diarrhea
- Lack of hunger for other nutritious food
- Stunted growth
- Obesity

So, to reduce these risks, use the majority of your juice in recipes or meals such as:

- Juice instead of water in oatmeal for a fruity flavor
- Mix yogurt & juice with a fork for a smoothie without a blender
- Use frozen juice concentrate to flavor yogurt
- Add juice (apple and orange) to marinades for meat
- Add juice to dressing for salads
- Add juice to sweeten soups
- Freeze in cups with sticks for popsicle snacks

Storage Tips

- Keep opened juice in the refrigerator and use with in a couple of weeks.
- Keep frozen concentrate frozen until use.

Bread   juice, milk, eggs

Applesauce Raisin Bread

Makes 1 loaf (12 servings)

Ingredients

    1 1/2 cups all-purpose flour
    1 1/2 tsp baking powder
    1/2 tsp baking soda
    1 1/2 tsp ground cinnamon
    1 cup quick cooking oats

    ¾ cup packed brown sugar
    ¾ cup raisins
    1 1/4 cups applesauce
    1/3 cup vegetable oil
    2 eggs, beaten*
    1/4 cup milk*
    1/4 cup apple juice*

*WIC food

Steps

1. Preheat oven to 350°.
2. y   Grease and flour an 8 1/2 x 4 1/2-inch loaf pan.
3. y   Soak raisins in apple juice.
4. y   In a large bowl, whisk together flour, baking powder, soda, cinnamon, oats, and brown sugar. Add applesauce, oil, eggs, and milk; stir until just combined. Mix in raisins.
5. y   Spread batter into prepared pan.
6. Bake for 55 to 60 minutes. Remove from pan immediately, and cool on a wire rack.

y   Steps for Children

Salad   juice

Tooty Fruity Salad

4 servings, about 1 cup each

Ingredients

    4 cups assorted fruit, cut into bite-sized pieces (such as banana, strawberries, apples, grapes, oranges, pineapple, etc.)

    1/4 cup shredded coconut

    1/4 cup orange juice* 1/4 cup vanilla yogurt

*WIC food

Steps

    1 . y   Put ingredients in bowl.

    2 . y   Mix.

y   Steps for Children

Meaty Vegetable Soup

Makes 6 servings

Ingredients

    1 1/2 lb ground meat (beef, turkey, wild game, etc.)

    4 cups frozen or fresh, cubed, cooked vegetables

    2 cups cooked noodles

    2 large cans V-8 juice*

    6 potatoes, peeled and cubed

    1 medium onion, chopped

    3 tbsp beef bouillon

    1/2 cup shredded cheese

*WIC food

Steps

1. In large soup pan combine V-8 juice, frozen veggies, potatoes, and beef bouillon.

2. Using the V-8 juice can, fill it half full with water and add this to the soup pan.

3. In a large skillet brown meat and onions.

4. When meat is medium brown, drain any extra liquid then add meat to soup pan. Add noodles and cook over medium heat about 1 1/2 to 2 hours.

5. Sprinkle cheese over top and serve

Main Dish   juice

Chicken with Orange Sauce

Makes 4 servings

Ingredients

- 4 skinless, boneless chicken breasts
- 1 tbsp vegetable oil
- **2 1/2 cups orange juice***
- 3 tbsp cornstarch
- 1/2 cup hot water
- 3 tbsp honey
- 1/4 tsp ground ginger (optional)

*WIC food

Steps

1. In a skillet, brown chicken breasts in 1 tablespoon oil over medium heat. Cook until chicken is done and juices run clear.
2. Add orange juice to the pan.
3. When juice just begins to bubble around the edges of the pan, add corn starch that has been dissolved in 1/4 cup hot water.
4. y   Mix ginger and honey together in a cup, and add to orange juice.
5. Cook until sauce is thick and slightly browned.
6. Serve over rice and enjoy!

y   Steps for Children

Dessert   juice, milk

Orange Creamsicles

Makes 4 popsicles

Ingredients

- **1 cup orange juice***
- **1/2 cup apple juice***
- 1 tsp honey
- 1/2 tsp vanilla
- **2 tbsp dry milk***
- 2 ice cubes

*WIC food

Also need

4 small paper cups or washed pudding containers
4 popsicle sticks or plastic spoons

Steps

1. y   Put all ingredients into a blender.
2. Blend until smooth.
3. y   Put into paper cups or pudding cups with popsicle sticks.
4. y   Cover with plastic wrap or aluminum foil.
5. Freeze overnight at least, but will last for a week
6. y   To serve take out of freezer and let sit, pop out and enjoy.

Got Milk?

Milk is also an excellent snack (children should have whole milk until 2 years, then low fat.)

- Milk is a great way to add calcium to any meal
- Use milk in drinks
- Use with cereal and fruit
- Use in frozen desserts and puddings
- Use in cream sauces
- Use in dressing to make them creamier
- Add to soups to make them creamier and thicker
- Use in gravies
- Add to ground meat meals (meat loaf, burgers)
- Add to mashed potatoes for a creamier taste
- Moisten chicken or fish before breading using cereal

Storage Tips

- Keep fresh milk refrigerated and covered at all times.
- Don't mix old and new milk.
- Keep unopened can of evaporated milk in a dry place.
- Keep powdered milk closed and in a cool, dry place.

Freezing Milk

Freezing is a great way to save milk for a couple of weeks after a big sale. Warning: thawed milk is perfectly safe and wholesome, but the texture might change a bit. To reduce texture change stir well after thawing.

To freeze — Remove at least 1 cup of milk from the top of the container so there is room for expansion. The milk should be frozen before the 'best if used by' date & will last for a month.

To thaw — Thaw milk in the refrigerator so it doesn't spoil. Make sure it is completely thawed. Mix well before using and use as soon as possible.

Snack   milk

Frozen Fruit Pops

Makes 8 pops

Ingredients

    2 cups fruit (peaches, strawberries, berries, etc.)

    2 bananas, peeled and cut in pieces

    1 (8 oz) cup flavored yogurt

    1 cup milk*

*WIC food

Also need

8 (7 ounce-size) paper cups or washed pudding containers

8 wooden craft/popsicle sticks or plastic spoons

Steps

1. Mash fruit with a fork. Add remaining ingredients. Stir until smooth. *(If using a blender, blend all ingredients together until smooth.)*
2. y   Fill cups 3/4 full with mixture.
3. y   Place wooden stick or plastic spoon in the middle of each cup.
4. Cover each cup with plastic wrap. Set cups in freezer for about 3 hours.
5. To serve, remove from freezer, let sit for about 10 minutes, and pull out of paper cups.

y   Steps for Children

Breakfast/Snack   milk

Banana-Ana Smoothie

4 servings

Ingredients

    2 cups fruit (such as banana, peach, strawberries, pineapple or berries)

    1 (8 oz) cup milk*

    1 cup ice cubes, if desired

    dash cinnamon, if desired

*WIC food

Steps

    1 . y   Put ingredients in blender.

    2. Cover blender and blend ingredients until smooth (about 3 minutes).

    3 . y   To serve, pour into cups

    4 . y   Top with a dash of cinnamon.

y   Steps for Children

soup   milk, egg

Potato Soup

Makes 6 servings

Ingredients

- 4 tbsp butter
- 2 large onions, finely chopped
- 2 tbsp flour
- 3 cups chicken broth
- 5 medium potatoes, peeled and diced into small cubes
- **3 cups milk***
- 1/2 cup frozen or canned green peas
- **3 eggs***
- 4 oz cream cheese, softened
- 1/4 cup chopped cilantro leaves (optional)

WIC food

Steps

1. Melt butter in large saucepan. Cook onions until soft but not brown.
2. Stir in flour and mix until smooth.
3. Add chicken broth gradually, stirring constantly until boiling.
4. Add potatoes, pepper, and salt, and simmer for 15 minutes.
5. Add milk and peas and continue cooking gently for 5 minutes.
6. Meanwhile beat eggs and cream cheese together in bowl, then gradually add 2 cups of the hot soup to the egg mixture, beating constantly to avoid curdling.
7. Return the contents of the bowl to the saucepan and heat through, but do not boil.
9. y   Serve with a garnish of cilantro.

Soup   milk

Three Little Pigs' Vegetable Soup

4 servings, about 1 cup each

Ingredients

- 2 tbsp vegetable oil
- 1 finely chopped onion
- 3 cups chopped vegetables, fresh or frozen (such as carrots, potatoes, broccoli, peas, green beans, corn, etc.)
- 2 cups vegetable broth or 2 cups water and 2 bouillon cubes
- **1 1/2 cups milk***

*WIC food

Steps

1. In large soup pot, heat oil over medium heat. Cook onion in oil for about 2 minutes or until soft and lightly browned.
2. Add vegetables and broth to pot.
3. Bring ingredients to a boil. Cover pot and simmer for 20-30 minutes.
4. Add milk. Stir until soup boils and thickens.

Main Dish								milk

Stroganoff

Makes 4 servings

Ingredients

- 1 tbsp vegetable oil
- 1/4 lb fresh mushrooms, sliced or 1 cup canned
- 1 large onion, sliced, 2 cups
- 2 tbsp all purpose flour
- **4 cups (1 quart) milk, at the boiling point * 1**
- tbsp powdered chicken stock seasoned base
- 2 tbsp Hungarian sweet paprika (optional)
- 1 tsp dried basil, crushed (optional)
- 1/2 tsp freshly ground black pepper
- 1/4 tsp ground nutmeg (optional)
- 1/8 tsp red pepper flakes (optional)
- 1 cup sour cream
- 2 cups cooked meat, cubed
- 4-5 cups cooked & drained pasta or rice

WIC food

Steps

1. Heat the oil in a large, non-stick skillet. Add the onions and sliced mushrooms and cook over medium heat, stirring frequently, until the onion is soft, about 12 minutes.

2. Add the flour to the skillet and cook, stirring constantly for 3 minutes.

3. Add the hot milk and chicken stock base and bring to a boil, stirring constantly.

4. Reduce the heat to low and simmer, stirring frequently, until slightly thickened, about 15 minutes.

5. Stir in the paprika, basil, black pepper, nutmeg, and red pepper flakes, then simmer for 5 minutes.

6,7. Stir in the sour cream and meat and serve immediately over the pasta or rice.

Dessert   milk

Rice Pudding

Serves 4

Ingredients

3 cups milk*
1 cup white rice (washed)
3/4 cup sugar
1 1/2 tbsp of vanilla extract
Handful dried fruit (raisins, dates, cranberries, etc.)
1 pinch of cinnamon (optional)

*WIC food

Steps

1. In a saucepan, bring milk and sugar to a boil.
2. Add rice and vanilla extract.
3. Cook at medium heat for 8 minutes.
4. Stir while heating until creamy and/or sticky.
5. Add dried fruit and stir for 2 minutes. Set aside for 10 minutes.
6. y   Garnish with cinnamon.

y   Steps for Children

Peanut Butter

Yummy Peanut Butter

Peanut butter can be part of a filling & energy providing snack. There are many ways to eat peanut butter

- Spread it on breads, bagels and crackers
- It is great as a dip for vegetables and fruit
- Put it into smoothies
- Plenty of desserts use peanut butter
- Add a dollop of peanut butter to your oatmeal
- Add to pancakes and waffles or spread on top
- Use in spreads with cream cheese, juice or chocolate
- Mix with popcorn
- Add to breads
- Use in sweet marinades for meat
- With chocolate as a dessert
- As a snack by the spoonful
- Sandwiches: eat with peanut butter
  The traditional: jelly/jam Bananas

    Tomatoes
    Apples & cinnamon
    Chocolate sauce
    Brown sugar Honey
    Powdered milk flavors or hot cocoa mix
    Cheese

Storage Tips

- Peanut butter does not need to be refrigerated, just keep in a dry place.
- Peanut butter can last up to one month after opening

Breakfast   peanut butter, milk, eggs, cereal

PB&J French Toast

Makes 4 sandwiches

Ingredients

8 slices whole wheat, white or other

1/4 cup peanut butter*

3 tbsp. jam

2 eggs*

2 tbsp. milk*

1/2 cups Post Honey Bunches of Oats Cereal, crushed* 2 cups sliced fresh fruit, such as strawberries or bananas, etc.

1 tbsp. sifted powdered sugar

1/2 cup maple syrup

*WIC food

Steps

1. Preheat oven to 350°F.
2. y   Make 4 peanut butter and jam sandwiches.
3. y   Break eggs into shallow dish. Add milk and beat with wire whisk for 30 seconds.
4. y   Place crushed cereal in pie plate.
5. y   Dip each sandwich into egg mixture, then into cereal, turning to evenly coat both sides. Press cereal gently into bread to secure.
6. y   Place on lightly greased baking sheet.
7. Bake 20 min. or until golden brown.
8. Cut each sandwich diagonally in half; top with fruit. Sprinkle with powdered sugar. Serve with syrup.

y   Steps for Children

Bread   peanut butter, milk, egg

Peanut Butter Banana Bread

Makes one loaf

Ingredients

2 1/2 cups all-purpose flour

1 cup sugar

3 1/2 tsp baking powder

1 cup mashed ripe bananas (2 to 3 medium)

3/4 cup crunchy peanut butter*

3/4 cup milk*

1/4 cup vegetable oil

1 egg*

*WIC food

Steps

1. Preheat oven to 350°F.

2. y   Grease 9 x 5 x 3-inch loaf pan.

3. y   Combine flour, sugar and baking powder in large bowl. Add banana, peanut butter, milk, oil and egg.

4. y   Mix just until blended. (Do not over-mix.)

5. Bake at 350°F for 60 to 65 minutes or until toothpick inserted in center comes out clean. (Cover top loosely with foil after 45 minutes to prevent over browning.) Cool 10 minutes in pan. Remove to cooling rack.

y   Steps for Children

Main Dish peanut butter

Chicken on a Stick

Serves 4

Ingredients

- 1/2 cup barbecue sauce
- **1/2 cup creamy peanut butter***
- 1/2 cup lime juice
- 4 tbsp chopped cilantro (optional)
- 1 lb boneless skinless chicken breasts, cut into strips
- 12 wooden skewers

WIC food

Steps

1. y Mix barbecue sauce, peanut butter, lime juice and cilantro in 2 resealable plastic bags.
2. y Add chicken and vegetables to different bags then seal.
3. y Turn bags over several times to evenly coat chicken and vegetables with the barbecue sauce mixture.
4. Refrigerate at least 1 hour or overnight to marinate.
5. Preheat grill to medium-high heat.
6. Remove chicken and vegetables from marinade; discard marinade. Thread chicken and vegetables onto skewers.
7. Grill 4 to 5 minutes on each side or until chicken and vegetables are cooked through.

y Steps for Children

Learn more about healthy living choices from your local WIC office. Look for these and other materials to help you take small steps that are good for the health of you and your family:

Play time... so good for me!

Play more...

- Dance and move to music.
- Play indoors and outdoors: hopscotch, hide-n-seek or make a marching band.
- Take a walk together.
- Let your baby crawl and explore safely.
- Encourage your children to be active
  —Let them play and have fun
  —jump rope, hula hoop, somersault
- Teach your children new skills
  —throw and kick a ball, shoot and dribble a basketball, swim

Sit Less...

- Turn off the TV one night a week.
- Add a 10-minute activity break for every hour you sit.
- Limit computer use and videogames

Water, Water... so good for me!

- Drink water between meals and at bedtime.

- Drink milk and 100% juice in a cup with meals and snacks:
  - 2 cups (16 oz) milk a day
    - Whole milk for children 1–2 years
    - 2% or less fat milk for children age 2 and older
  - ½ – ¾ cup (4–6 oz) juice or less a day

- Limit soda, Kool-aid, Tang, fruit drinks and sport drinks.

- Drink water with fluoride to prevent tooth decay.

- Ask your dentist or healthcare provider about flouride.

- Drink water to prevent fatigue.

- Thirst is often mistaken for hunger.

My Favorite Recipes

My Favorite Recipes

My Favorite Recipes

My Favorite Recipes

My Favorite Recipes

S.S. Publishing